The 5 Habits of Deeply Contented People

Andrew Page

VTR
Publications

ISBN 978-3-95776-009-8

Cover design and illustrations: Chris Allcock

Printed by Lightning Source

Contents

Acknowledgements

I am grateful to Chris Allcock for the drawings and for the cover design, and especially to Thomas Mayer for agreeing to publish this book.

I thank those who read the manuscript and gave me their feedback and encouragement: James and Nicola Musson, Helen Savage, Jo Simpkins and Wolfgang Widmann.

This book is dedicated to all those who are willing to try out the habits for themselves. To God be the glory!

Andrew Page
andrew@themarkdrama.com

Introduction

The Search for Contentment

Most people are looking for contentment, and the reason some people are not looking is that they have given up.

It's a basic human longing. But there are two problems.

First, it's in short supply. We may once have found contentment somewhere, but then we were disappointed. It might even be true, in the words of Henry David Thoreau, that most people *live lives of quiet desperation*.

And second, we often look for it in the wrong places. Sometimes it's in alcohol or some other drug; or we become workaholics; or we eat too much fine food.

I'm sure you can add to the list. It's long.

But these things don't work. At best, they are anaesthetics to help us forget the contentment we long for but can't find. They take the pain away without solving the problem.

So why is this longing there?

The first chapter of the Bible says it's because we've been made in the image of God. That isn't meant in a physical sense.

What it *does* mean is that all of us have certain characteristics because we are created in God's image. Animals don't do these things (at least not in the way we do), because God didn't make them in his image when he created them.

There is something special about us human beings.

Now here's where it gets interesting. If we can find out what these things are, and start to actively put them into practice, *we will be being truly ourselves*.

And that will mean that we are more contented.

That's what this book is about.

Part One is called **Discovering the 5 Habits**. We will look at the habits which express the image of God in human beings and which are to be found in the second chapter of the Bible book of Genesis.

As we examine each habit we will first *read the Bible*, looking at Adam in Genesis chapter 2 and seeing what he does. We will notice that each habit is a reflection of who God is.

Next we will *think it through*, to see what it might mean for us to put this habit into practice. I will provide examples of what each habit might look like for us, although in the end each of us will have to make our own decision as to what that will mean in our own experience.

And then I will encourage all of us to *try it out*. There is no point in thinking about these 5 habits if we don't have a go at them for ourselves.

And if we do, we will discover that they bring contentment with them.

There are at least four possible objections to Part One of this book. One or two of them may apply to you.

Objection One

'But I don't believe in God.'

Thanks for your honesty.

But it's still true, isn't it, that you look for contentment? And of course I am making the bold claim that because we're all made in God's image these 5 habits work for everyone, whether they believe in God or not.

So I hope you will read on and try them anyway. I'm not asking you to pretend that you believe God exists, just to give these 5 habits a try. You have nothing to lose.

And a lot to gain.

And here's Objection Two:

Objection Two

'But I can't take the Genesis creation account literally.'

I'm not asking you to.

Christians have different views as to how literally we should take the first three chapters of Genesis. For example: did God create everything in six literal days, or did he use an evolutionary process in order to make the world and the universe?

And does Genesis chapter 2 contain symbolic language, or is it to be taken literally?

What *all* Christians agree on is that God created everything. *How* he did it is less important than *that* he did it.

And *all* Christians believe that God made human beings in his image. It makes sense to think about what that can mean for us in our own experience.

Objection Three

'But hasn't the Fall destroyed the image of God in us?'

Genesis chapter 3, which is the chapter immediately after the chapter we are looking at in this book, tells us about Adam and Eve's rebellion against God's authority.

But although the Fall may have *damaged* the image of God in us, it hasn't *destroyed* it. The Bible says that all human beings have still *been made in God's likeness* (James 3:9).

So there's some repair work to be done. But every human being is made in God's image.

And Objection Four is very important.

Objection Four

'Are you saying these 5 habits are going to solve all my problems?'

No, I'm not. All of us have struggles: it's part of life in a broken world.

If, for example, your family has faced great tragedy it may be that it feels like there's a wall there every day barring the way to contentment.

Or if you suffer from depression you may need help through medication, or expert psychotherapy or counselling.

So these 5 habits are not a miracle cure for anything.

But I am convinced that everyone who tries them out will experience a deeper level of contentment. We all start from a different place, but all of us can experience more joy and peace than we do now.

If we do try putting these habits into practice we may be surprised that the Bible is so practical! And this may prompt us to take a fresh look at whether the Christian faith can be taken seriously.

So **Part Two** is called **Discovering God**. It's much shorter than Part One and tells us what the Bible says about Jesus revealing God to us and offering us a friendship with him.

Some of us may reject this out of hand. Others may have questions they want to follow up, and still others may decide that they believe that what the Christian faith says about Jesus is true. If you come into either of these two categories, Appendix 1 is the place to go.

For people who have made the decision to trust in Jesus and follow him, there is something else in the second chapter of the Bible which is worth putting into practice.

That's why **Part Three** is called **Discovering the Missing Habit**.

Once again we will *read the Bible* to find this habit in Genesis chapter 2 and *think it through* to consider the practical implications for us. And then, of course, I will encourage us to *try it out*.

We will see that this habit, too, leads to contentment. And, if we do try it out we will *experience* this contentment in our own lives.

I hope you will enjoy the habits of deeply contented people!

Part One

Discovering the 5 Habits

The habits we are looking at in this first part of the book are all to be found in Genesis chapter 2.

But what's the big deal? Why am I expecting to find something important about human beings in this chapter?

The reason is because of something Genesis tells us in the previous chapter's creation account. The writer tells us that *God created mankind in his own image* (Genesis 1:27).

But that leaves every reader with a question: what does it *mean* for us that we are created in God's image?

The obvious place for us to look for an answer to the question is Genesis chapter 2. The man, who is called Adam (see 20), *does* certain things which give us an insight into what the image of God in human beings looks like.

Theologians have written a vast amount about the image of God, much of it technical and complicated. You may want to follow this up on a more academic level.

But in Part One we are looking at the image of God in us by focusing on the 5 habits described in Genesis 2. Ever since I first saw them I have been finding out what they mean for me, with my style and personality.

And as I have put them into practice I have experienced a deeper contentment.

This does not mean that I am always deeply contented! But using these habits has certainly increased my contentment levels.

I hope you will try them too.

Habit 1: Enjoy beauty

We all have different ideas, of course, as to what's beautiful. But you won't find a person on the planet who is not enthusiastic about beauty. This first habit, like all the others, is part of what it means to be in God's image: it's one of the things which make us truly human. And therefore deeply contented.

Now the Lord God had planted a garden in the east, in Eden; and there he put the man he had formed. The Lord God made all kinds of trees grow out of the ground – trees that were pleasing to the eye and good for food.

Genesis 2:8-9a

Read the Bible

So God has planted a garden, and the man (he's called Adam, see 20) is living there.

The writer doesn't tell us what the garden looked like, but he does mention that God made sure there were trees. We don't get a description of the trees, either.

The writer could just have told us that there were *trees that were good for food*. But before telling us that, he wants us to know that they were *pleasing to the eye* (9). So these trees were beautiful.

And whose eye are we talking about here? Well, there isn't much choice! This is about Adam, who has just been mentioned (8). For him the trees are not just offering potential meals, they are also a sight for sore eyes: they look beautiful.

And the theme of beauty doesn't stop there.

There's a paragraph in Genesis chapter 2 which I have always secretly been bored by. See how you react:

> *A river watering the garden flowed from Eden; from there it was separated into four headwaters. The name of the first is the Pishon; it winds through the entire land of Havilah, where there is gold. (The gold of that land is good; aromatic resin and onyx are also there.) The name of the second river is the Gihon; it winds through the entire land of Cush. The name of the third river is the Tigris; it runs along the east side of Ashur. And the fourth river is the Euphrates.*
> Genesis 2:10-14

Although I used to find that boring I have changed my mind.

I think the existence of these rivers should convince us of something. Four rivers means there is no shortage of irrigation. And that tells us two things about the garden.

First, the trees and the other vegetation can develop and grow: they are not going to be stunted by lack of water.

And second, the animals God has created (and which will appear later in chapter 2 – see verses 19 and 20) are going to be getting all the food and drink they need.

The message is clear. The Garden of Eden is *beautiful*; and Adam, before he even starts thinking about things like diet, is *enjoying the beauty*.

And, I dare say, feeling deeply contented.

If enjoying beauty is part of what it means to be made in God's image, we can expect that God, too, takes pleasure in beautiful things.

And that is exactly what we find at the end of the first chapter of the Bible.

At the end of the description of everything that has been created we read that *God saw all that he had made, and it was very good* (Genesis 1:31).

Do you get the picture? I can't prove this, but I think the words *it was very good* suggest that this is not a dry, dispassionate judgment on God's part, but an expression of pleasure.

God was enjoying the beauty of what he had created and feeling contented. Which is why we should enjoy beauty, too, in order to become the contented people we were designed to be.

Think it through

What springs to mind when you think of beauty? What are you imagining as you read this?

It may be nature, which is what it was in Adam's case. You can get lost just by looking at a rose and seeing the drops of dew on the petals.

Or it's the view when walking your dog along a coastal path. You gaze at the expanse of the sea and the sky, and you marvel at where they meet on the horizon.

It makes you *feel* something.

It's being in the Alps, surrounded by snow-covered mountains, when you can make out mountain range after mountain range stretching far into the distance.

When you see a cantering horse the word which comes to mind is *beautiful*. Its legs are working in perfect harmony and its mane is flowing in the wind.

Or it's going for a walk on the common, watching the ducks on the pond, being surprised at the way the leaves change colour from day to day.

It may be music. You often have music on in the background, but when you hear certain tracks from your favourite band or sections from a piano concerto you wish you'd written yourself, you feel pleasure.

You can remember when you first heard this music, and when you hear it today you're glad you're alive.

Or it's going to a concert and being spellbound, astonished at the music and its effect on you. The music is beautiful and the feeling you get listening to it is beautiful too.

It may be the solution to a mathematical problem. It all looks impossible at first sight, but the solution, once seen, is elegant and beautiful.

It makes your heart beat faster: you're excited, you're experiencing pleasure.

It may be art. You can spend a large part of the day in a gallery: just looking. Some of your friends think it's a waste of time, but you are amazed at the beauty of what you see.

And there are some paintings you stand in front of for a long time. The colours combine to create an atmosphere, and the technique almost takes your breath away.

You may not be able to explain to anyone else the way the painting is impacting you. But you are *enjoying beauty*.

It may be books. Perhaps it's a classic novel from a different century and a different culture; or a bestselling modern thriller.

But you lose all sense of time when you are reading certain books, and you re-read some chapters because you are in awe at the skill with which the author describes certain emotions or events.

It may be films. Some of your friends just love a great story. You do too, but you are also enjoying the way this film has been cast and directed.

And there are moments which bring tears to your eyes: a camera angle, the juxtaposition of a word from one character and a look from another.

You are enjoying beauty.

Do any of these things resonate with you? I may have mentioned something which is exactly what gets you enjoying beauty. Or something you have read has reminded you of what *does* fill you with joy.

As you have been reading this section you may have been thinking 'Why doesn't he mention great architecture?'; or 'What gets me going is beautifully designed fabrics'; or 'How can anyone *not* be moved by the majesty of a polar bear?'

Please think it through. What does *Enjoy beauty* mean for you? As a human being you are made in God's image and the enjoyment of beauty is part of what makes you *you*.

But what's important is that we don't just accept the principle, but realise in practice what kind of beauty we respond to.

You may have known this already, though you may have thought of something else while reading this.

Try it out

Well, you probably already have.

But is there some way in which you could enjoy beauty every day?

Often there isn't much beauty in our lives: maybe we face tough situations in our family or at work. Which is why we need to deliberately expose ourselves to beauty, wherever we find it.

And I can guarantee something.

If we will build into our day opportunities to enjoy beauty, we will feel more contented because we will be doing what people made in God's image do.

Please try Habit 1. Make it part of every day and deep contentment will be more and more part of you.

Habit 1: Something to do

Do you know what kinds of beauty you enjoy most?

If the enjoyment of beauty is not already a regular (daily?) part of your life, what steps can you take to change the situation?

And if you believe God exists, why not take some time to thank him for the beautiful things which fill your heart with joy and contentment?

Habit 2: Dig your garden

This habit doesn't have to be about gardening! When God put Adam in the Garden of Eden he gave him a job to do: looking after where he was. People who don't commit to this second habit are much less likely to be contented, because they are not behaving like they are made in God's image. But people who do will re-discover what contentment is.

The Lord God took the man and put him in the Garden of Eden to work it and take care of it.

Genesis 2:15

Read the Bible

Sometimes it's fascinating what the Bible *doesn't* say.

It doesn't say that God put Adam in the Garden of Eden *to relax on a recliner and sip cool drinks with umbrellas in them.*

What it *does* say is that Adam had some work to do, which is what Genesis chapter 1 has already told us. After God created human beings, he told them to *fill the earth and subdue it* (Genesis 1:28).

That word *subdue* doesn't mean *ransack* or *subjugate* (although sometimes we have behaved as if it did). It means *take charge* and *cultivate*. Adam is not meant to be passive; instead he is to be pro-actively at work in the world God has put him in.

So that is what's happening in chapter 2. God puts Adam in the garden first to enjoy it (8-9), and second to look after it (15). That's what the second habit is.

Let's be clear that this is not God's Plan B: it is part of his design for human beings right from the start. There's no way Adam felt frustrated at being given this work to do: as he looked after the garden he wasn't thinking that he was wasting his time.

My guess is that Adam was planting, digging and pruning. And that he was contented as he did these things.

If actively working in this way is part of what it means to be made in God's image, then you'd expect that God is a worker too.

And that's exactly what we find at the beginning of Genesis chapter 2.

The writer tells us: *By the seventh day God had finished the work he had been doing* (2). So it's right to talk about the *work* of creation and to conclude that *we* should be workers because *God* is a worker.

There's a clue to something else here too.

The fact that God didn't work on uninterruptedly means that we shouldn't either: *Then God blessed the seventh day and made it holy, because on it he rested from all the work of creating that he had done* (3).

This is going to help us to understand Habit 2. This job of *digging our garden* (whatever that means in practice) is not to be all-consuming:

God is not a hard taskmaster running us into the ground. Yes, he gives us work to do; but he also tells us we need rest and recreation.

Just as God was active in creating the garden, so we are designed to be active, too, in looking after it. If you and I take time to dig our garden we will know the contentment we were designed to experience.

Think it through

It's a vicious circle, really.

If I am feeling down I can very easily end up not doing anything. And if I am not doing anything I end up feeling even more down.

I suspect most of us recognise this pattern.

So what does it mean to dig my garden? As we've already seen, it means looking after and taking care of where we are. There are at least three things this means in practice.

My garden is where I live. So I'm talking about my room, my flat or my house. Visit someone who is feeling very low, and it may well be that where they live is a tip.

When I am feeling down I lack energy. But here's something that helps. I go to the kitchen and clear out *one* of the kitchen cupboards. I wipe the inside of the cupboard with a damp cloth and put everything back neatly in its place.

And I *always* feel better for it. It's only taken me 10 minutes, and of course it hasn't solved all my problems. But it has lifted my spirits.

The reason is simple: I have been digging my garden. It's Habit 2.

Another option about where you live is your desk (or the table you use as a desk). Sometimes it's just one huge piling system, except that it isn't a system. And it's *depressing*: you can't find that bill you know you should be paying or you last saw your diary a few weeks ago.

So digging your garden means tidying your desk.

But don't do it the wrong way! The wrong way to tidy a desk is to take the first piece of paper off the top of one of the piles: you bin it or file it or write an email to whoever gave it to you.

Then you move on to piece of paper number 2.

This takes ages: after half an hour the piles look as high as they were at the beginning. This is not a recipe for things *looking* up; it's a recipe for you *giving* up.

Here's the right way to tidy a desk.

Put all the piles of paper on to some chairs or even on to the floor. Dust and polish the desk: you are already doing Habit 2. And you will feel better already.

Now pick up the top piece of paper from one of the piles and put it into one of 3 new piles: a to-do pile, a rubbish pile and a filing pile. Do the same with every piece of paper. You will feel even better.

Now throw away the rubbish pile. You could just dump it all in a cardboard box, but it's even better to get it off the premises: go outside and throw it all in the recycling. You will feel better again.

Now is the time to file all the stuff in the filing pile. Put everything in its proper place and you will feel better (and *I'm* feeling better just describing the process!).

There's only one pile left now: the to-do stuff. You probably won't get that all done at once, but you can make a start. And even making a start will lift your spirits.

Why does this work? It works because it is Habit 2: you are digging your garden.

And of course something else you can do to dig your garden is to dig your garden! I am very relieved that I live in a flat because it means that I never have to do any gardening at all: but maybe you are the kind of person who will feel better after gardening, even if it's only for 20 minutes.

Maybe this would work for me too. But as things stand I have no intention of finding out!

So my garden is where I live. But there's more.

My garden is my body. If I get almost no exercise I am not digging my garden. And this will be a downward spiral: the longer I avoid exercise the harder it will be for me to start.

This is not about all of us training to run a marathon. It will be for some people of course.

But for most of us it may just be regularly going for a brisk 30-minute walk. Or it's taking the decision to join a gym or go to a dance class, or to meet up with a friend once a week to play tennis.

If I get regular exercise I will feel more content, and that is because I will be digging my garden.

But I won't feel content if I am over-eating. This doesn't mean that I only eat health-foods (though some of us may make that decision); it just means being sensible about what I eat and how much of it I eat.

If my body is part of my garden, then it makes sense to look after it. Just as Adam looked after the garden God had put him in, so we need to care for where God has put us.

And all of us are living in a body.

My garden is also my work. If you have a job, doing it as well as you can is part of digging your garden, whether you like the job or not.

Your work may be cooking for the family and looking after the children, or it may mean working in an office or a factory. But *do it well.*

And if you don't have a job for whatever reason, but have time to kill, why not get work in a charity shop a few days a week? You will feel more contented: you will feel more like you are *living* and less like you are *being lived*.

Try it out

We have been thinking about Habit 2.

Here are some things to think about.

Habit 2: Something to do

In what ways would you say you are already digging your garden?

In what ways do you want to start digging your garden *as far as where you live is concerned?*

In what ways do you want to start digging your garden *as far as your body is concerned?*

And in what ways do you want to start digging your garden *as far as your work life is concerned?*

And if you believe God exists, why not take some time to ask him to help you to dig the garden he has given you?

Please be sure of this: as you take steps to dig your garden you will feel better. It won't solve all your problems; but you will experience a deeper contentment.

Guaranteed.

Habit 3: Practise self-control

This is the habit most of us don't like the sound of! However, to different degrees we all do this, and we're sorry for people who have a massive struggle in this area. Being made in God's image means that we can make decisions as to what we do and what we don't do. And when we do practise self-control we always feel the benefits.

And the Lord God commanded the man: 'You are free to eat from any tree in the garden; but you must not eat from the tree of the knowledge of good and evil, for when you eat from it you will certainly die.'

Genesis 2:16-17

Read the Bible

One reason why these are not everyone's favourite Genesis chapter 2 sentences is that they're negative.

But look closely at them and you'll see that this divine command is actually very positive too.

First, of all the trees in the garden there's only one which is a no-go area for Adam: otherwise he can eat anything he likes (16). The writer is introducing us to a God who is unbelievably generous.

And second, the forbidden tree is not surrounded by a concrete wall to make access impossible (17). Instead, God is giving Adam the freedom to *decide for himself* not to eat from it. God hasn't made a robot: he's made a *person*.

So Adam can decide to practise self-control.

Now if that is part of what it means to be made in God's image, you'd expect God to have the same characteristic. And that's exactly what we find when we look at the first few chapters of the Bible.

In Genesis chapter 1 it's God who decides what he is going to create: the ideas come from his mind and the power to do it is all his. He is the free agent to end all free agents.

And in Genesis chapter 3, after the people he has created have misused their freedom to disobey his command, God exercises self-control again: he decides to judge but not to destroy.

So self-control reminds us that we're made in God's image. That's why it gives us a good feeling.

Ask an athlete. The training is sometimes incredibly hard and it involves *not* doing some things she would often love to say *Yes* to; but the sense of satisfaction is worth all the self-control.

Ask a chess-player. Studying books written by a Grand Master is hard work and means there may not be time for some other things; but the progress and success this brings result in a deep contentment.

And ask a student. Revising for exams or writing a dissertation involves self-control, especially on those days he doesn't feel like it. But ask him how he feels when the exam is passed or the dissertation is finished, and his smile will tell you more than his words.

Self-control is a theme that runs through the whole Bible story. It doesn't make us *less* human; it makes us *more* human.

One reason parents should discipline their children is this: if we don't experience discipline while growing up we'll never manage *self*-discipline as adults.

So practising self-control isn't something negative. Instead it increases our sense of self-worth and contentment.

Habit 3 *works.*

Think it through

Moral decision-making is only one area in which we need self-control.

Even if you don't believe God exists, you believe in right and wrong. You use the word *ought*, don't you?

You almost certainly think that love is better than hate; and you think there are some things people *shouldn't* do.

Doing some things gives you a bad feeling (whether or not you call this *conscience*). And *not* doing those things gives you a good feeling.

Let's think of some practical examples, first of things which could hardly be described as moral issues at all.

It's a hot day and you have brought your food shopping into the kitchen and put it away. You fancy a bowl of ice-cream. Fine.

But after you've finished that one you want a second. Why not? You've just brought home enough to allow you to spend the next hour solidly eating ice-cream.

You know this is true: if you do eat 3 bowlfuls of ice-cream you will enjoy the experience at the time but feel a failure later. And though you may struggle to limit yourself to one bowlful you know you will feel better for it afterwards.

There are a number of things which offer themselves as short-cuts to contentment. Too much ice-cream is one of them.

But there are plenty of others.

Too much alcohol. Internet porn. Pigging out on chocolate. Addiction to anything.

Does any of that ring bells for you? All of these things (and many others) offer contentment. But if they do provide it, it's only short-term: afterwards come the regret and the emptiness.

And we all know from experience that saying *No* to any of these things results in inner satisfaction and deep contentment.

The mention of internet porn has already moved us into the realm of moral issues. And once again, self-control brings massive benefits.

It occurs to you that you could save yourself some money by failing to declare some of your income to the tax authorities. Why not?

Someone offers you an easy way of cheating in an important exam coming up soon. Everyone does it, don't they?

You are presented with an opportunity to begin an adulterous relationship. It's so easy just to let things slip – a lie to your spouse or partner, the *It'll only happen once* excuse, or the biggest lie of all: *No one will ever know.*

If you believe that God exists you have to face the fact that *he* knows. And the stark truth is that *you* will know and that contentment will only be a word to you.

Now imagine yourself in the situation of having made the decision to complete your tax forms honestly: you may have a little less money, but won't you feel better?

If you go for the option of more revision instead of dishonesty, there will be a sense of satisfaction, won't there?

And if you decide to say *No* to the adulterous relationship, you will miss the pleasure and excitement which it was offering you; but won't you *feel* better?

On a number of issues we will have differences of opinion about what is right and what is wrong.

But on this we can agree: practising self-control will result in a deep sense of contentment. Experience tells us this, and common sense teaches it too.

Part of being made in God's image is the exercise of self-control. It was for Adam and it is for us.

This may be about moral issues or it may be about much less serious things.

But practising Habit 3 *always* leads to contentment.

Try it out

I'm sure that there are some areas in which you are already practising self-control. I hope you see that this is not a negative thing, but rather an act of freedom which brings dignity and contentment.

Habit 3: Something to do

What are the areas in which you already practise self-control? What benefits are you experiencing?

Has it occurred to you that there are other areas where controlling yourself would be the right thing for you to do? Which?

If you believe in God you might like to ask him to help you to practise self-control, particularly in areas where you struggle most.

And you might like to ask a friend to support you in this, by asking you from time to time how you are doing with self-control in a specific area.

If Habit 3 has impacted you and you have decided to make a new start with self-control in specific areas as a result of reading this chapter, please be expecting something.

Because, as you live like someone made in God's image, it's yours.

Contentment.

Habit 4: Be creative

Creativity is something we prize in others but often claim not to have ourselves. The problem is that lots of us have never discovered (or have forgotten) what it is that gets our creative juices flowing. But creativity, as a key part of what it means to be made in God's image, is a habit which can surprise us with the contentment it brings.

Now the Lord God had formed out of the ground all the wild animals and all the birds in the sky. He brought them to the man to see what he would name them; and whatever the man called each living creature, that was its name.

Genesis 2:19

Read the Bible

This is the part of Genesis chapter 2 which makes me smile.

Instead of just labelling the animals, God brings them to Adam and asks *him* to decide what they are to be called. It's almost as if God is excited to see how Adam reacts: *he brought them to the man to see what he would name them* (19).

So I imagine Adam being presented with a small bird, scratching his head and saying *Tiger?*

This is extraordinary stuff. In the first two chapters of the Bible God is depicted as being the only Creator of everything. And now here, before chapter 2 is finished, God is inviting Adam to be creative.

And there is no suggestion that Adam is unhappy about this: he doesn't tell God that he isn't up to it or try to wriggle out of the responsibility. Instead, his creative juices are flowing: he gets on with the job.

As we noted with Habit 3, we see here that God has not created a robot but a person. And being a person involves creativity.

If being creative is part of what it means to be made in God's image, we would expect that God, too, is creative.

And how.

According to the Bible God spoke words and everything came into existence. His creativity includes the intricate design of everything he has made; his limitless power made sure these things did not just remain in his imagination but became reality.

Sure, human beings cannot create something out of nothing. But we have astonishing powers to use what is already there to make new things.

Look at this short extract from an incredibly long list, and be astonished: cars, computers, poems, clothes, novels, cakes, space travel, photography, architecture, medicine, drama…

So creativity is part of our humanity.

The writer of Genesis repeats himself because he wants us to get the message: *So the man gave names to all the livestock, the birds in the sky and all the wild animals* (20).

The Bible says that all of us are creative. What's important is that we recognise that and find out the area we are creative in.

When someone discovers their area of creativity – and uses it – they discover a new joy and contentment. The reason is simple: they are experiencing something that is a part of what it means for them to be human.

Welcome to Habit 4!

Think it through

Some people know immediately where their creativity lies; others of us have no idea.

The big danger is that if we are in the second category we conclude that we are not creative at all.

Ask a roomful of people to raise their hands if they are creative, and less than half will do so. Try it and see.

Someone once said that most of us have the creativity educated out of us. They may be right.

It's certainly true that children are creative. Sometimes they produce drawings which only their parents will be impressed by; but nothing stops them being creative. Plan to put on a play with small children and you will not be short of volunteers.

As we become adults some of us seem to lose our creativity. But if we take Habit 4 seriously we will start searching.

One way of doing this is to ask friends or family in what way they consider us creative. But we need to be searching ourselves too.

If you are into cryptic crosswords, that is you being creative. Or perhaps there are other kinds of problems you enjoy solving.

But let me suggest some other possibilities. One or more of them may fit you perfectly. Or, as you read the next few paragraphs you may find yourself thinking something like this: *I'm not creative in that way; what gets me excited is...*

So see what strikes you.

Why not go to a dance class? Or do an Open University degree? Or decide to learn a language?

Would you consider teaching someone to read? Or writing a short story? Or taking (or giving) guitar lessons?

How about redecorating your lounge? You will use your creativity as you work out what you want the colours and the materials to be; and you will use your creativity as you actually do the work, too.

I have a friend who struggles with depression. Sometimes he needs medication, but something else which helps him is writing poetry. He may or may not ever show the poem to anyone else, but simply writing it lifts his spirits. It *works*.

So why not write a song? Or write a letter by hand to an old friend? Or decide to find out as much as you can about Italy?

How about joining a choir or auditioning for an amateur theatre group? What about choosing an author and deciding to read everything she's ever written?

The extraordinary thing about creativity is that it produces the contentment I am talking about in this book.

One of my favourite films is about a ballet of Stravinsky's *The Rite of Spring* rehearsed and performed mainly by school students. They got the volunteers because it was a change from normal boring school life, but there was opposition because many of the students didn't want the hard work involved.

But they produced a wonderful performance. And afterwards you could see the result on their faces: they had grown together as a group and were experiencing a joy they had not known before.

Can you remember a similar experience, after you appeared in a play or a musical performance, or after you wrote something you had worked hard to produce?

You may have dismissed it as unimportant because it wasn't part of an exam syllabus; but it wasn't. You had been creative, either alone or with others, and the aftermath was joy.

Creativity leads to contentment because it is part of what makes us human beings.

Try it out

If you can think of an area in which you are already being creative, be grateful.

If you can't, please don't fall for the trap of thinking that you're just not creative.

It's a lie. If you're a member of the human race you *are* creative. No doubt about it.

Habit 4: Something to do

If you know of an area in which you are already being creative, write that down. What steps are you taking to express that creativity?

Have you thought of a new area (whether mentioned above or not) in which you might be creative? If so, what will be your next steps in order to try this out?

If you feel uncreative and have no ideas about what might fit you, talk to family and/or friends to find out what ideas they have.

And if you believe that God exists, why not ask him to help you to understand more clearly how he has made you and how you can express creativity?

Habit 4, like all the others, is unbelievably important.

Being creative – or taking steps towards being creative – will lead to you having a firmer foundation and a deeper contentment.

Habit 5: Embrace others

This habit fills a gap left by the other four. In theory we could put those habits into practice in splendid isolation: this fifth habit stresses that we are made for relationship. In Genesis chapter 2 the emphasis is on marriage, but all friendship is a gift from God. It is part of what makes us truly human and opens the door to contentment.

Then the Lord God made a woman from the rib he had taken out of the man, and he brought her to the man. The man said, 'This is now bone of my bones and flesh of my flesh. She shall be called "woman", for she was taken out of man.'

Genesis 2:22-23

Read the Bible

The second chapter of Genesis makes it clear that God is against loneliness: *The Lord God said, It is not good for the man to be alone* (18).

This sentence is followed by the description of the animals being brought to Adam which we looked at when we were thinking about Habit 4.

It's almost like this is a test: is this going to solve Adam's aloneness problem? The answer is No: *But for Adam no suitable helper was found* (20b).

God's solution is the creation of the woman (21-22). The word *helper* doesn't imply any inferiority on Eve's part: she is not there to be Adam's slave but to be Adam's partner and friend.

You can tell that from the way Adam launches into poetry when he meets her! *The man said, This is now bone of my bones and flesh of my flesh; she shall be called 'woman', for she was taken out of man* (23).

The same topic turns the writer of Genesis into a poet in chapter 1: *So God created mankind in his own image, in the image of God he created them; male and female he created them* (27).

In the context of Genesis chapter 2 this is talking about marriage, as the writer makes clear: *That is why a man leaves his father and mother and is united to his wife, and they become one flesh* (24).

But most friendships don't result in marriage; whether we are married or not we all need people in our lives we can be close to. Whether it is literal or not, all of us need to embrace others.

If embracing others is part of what it means to be made in God's image, then we can expect that God is also into relationships.

And that's exactly what we find.

The Bible introduces us to God as a trinity — Father, Son and Holy Spirit. And it stresses two things: these are three distinct personalities, but together they make one God.

If we struggle to get our heads around this, then it is worth saying that it would be strange if we, as creatures, could fully and easily understand our Creator.

But do you see what this means?

Even before creating anything God was already experiencing relationship and is still doing so: the Father loves the Son and the Spirit, the Son loves the Father and the Spirit, and the Spirit loves the Father and the Son.

So embracing others is fundamental to *our* identity as human beings because embracing others is fundamental to *God's* identity.

This is why love is so important to us. Most of us want to get married and all of us value friendship; films and songs about love are a key ingredient in our culture; a life without love sounds to most of us more like a living death.

The New Testament goes so far as to say that God *is* love (1 John 4:16), in other words that love is at the centre of his being. It's at the centre of ours too.

Which is why we need to embrace others.

When God commands us to love one another, he is asking people he has made in his image to do what he does himself.

And it *works*.

Think it through

Every human being feels the need to embrace others. Sometimes the solution to aloneness for some people is to have a dog or a cat they can relate to.

That's great. But it is, at best, only a partial solution. As beings made in God's image we need relationships with others made in God's image if we are to find the quality of contentment we need.

The first area to think about is marriage, because that is the focus in Genesis chapter 2.

Husbands and wives should love one another and communicate that in words and actions. How this works out in practice will differ from couple to couple, but the principle is clear: husband and wife should embrace each other.

If both partners in a marriage are Christians I think they should be praying together. I knew a man who prayed with other people but never with his wife, although she longed for it to happen. Their marriage was strong in many ways, but she felt an inner frustration.

When it came to their 25th wedding anniversary, the couple exchanged presents, as they did every year. The wife watched as her husband unwrapped her present and waited for him to give her his.

But instead he said to her: *I know I've hurt you by not praying with you all these years. I am sorry. My present to you today is that I commit to praying with you every day in all the years God gives us together.*

But this is just one example of the principle in practice: husband and wife should embrace each other.

If you have children, do you show them *and tell them* that they matter to you? *If* you do, and *as* you do, you will experience contentment. And they will too.

But this is not just about family relationships.

If I am feeling down I may not feel much like seeing anyone else. But then I phone a friend and suggest meeting up for an hour for a coffee. When I get home from town I *always* feel better: I have embraced someone.

That's just one possibility among many.

If I send a card to a friend thanking them for their friendship or to say I hope their hospital appointment goes well, it won't only do *them* good; it will do *me* good too.

Inviting a few people in for a meal is another way of embracing others. This is not about me impressing them with my extraordinary culinary skills, but about inviting them to share an ordinary meal with me: by doing this I am communicating that they matter to me.

I will be tired afterwards; but I will feel good too.

Another possibility is to leave a small present in front of someone's front door: it won't only do *them* good.

We all have some people in our lives who don't qualify as friends, but we know them nevertheless. They may be work colleagues or they may be neighbours.

A friend of mine got a job in an office where no one said *Good morning* when they arrived at work or offered to make a coffee for anyone else. He started behaving differently: he was embracing his colleagues.

And people's behaviour in the office started to change.

But all this doesn't just apply to relationships with family, friends and acquaintances.

The way I thank the shopworker at the checkout or say hi to the bus driver communicates something too: it's another example of embracing people (but not in the literal sense!).

So we've looked at four areas in which Habit 5 can be put into practice: we can embrace family, friends, acquaintances and strangers.

Try it out

I'm sure you are already embracing others. But ask yourself these questions...

Habit 5: Something to do

What could you do this week to *embrace* members of your family in a new way?

How could you show love to one or more friends in the next few days?

In what way could you *embrace* some work colleagues or neighbours?

And why not decide to treat people differently the next time you go to the shops? What might this mean in practice?

I suggest you share some of these ideas with a good friend, who can ask you how you have been getting on with making your decisions reality.

And if you believe that God exists, you might like to ask him to help you embrace others.

All five of the habits we have been looking at are important.

But Habit 5 takes us to the core of our personhood. Love is one of the things which make us human beings. As we embrace others we are embracing ourselves too: we are being the people we were meant to be.

The 5 habits we have found in Genesis chapter 2 only work if we use them. Take a few minutes to think them through:

Enjoy beauty
Dig your garden
Practise self-control
Be creative
Embrace others

Which of these were you already doing before you started reading this book?

Which habit(s) would you do well to take steps to put into practice? What steps are you going to take?

Please remember: taking this seriously will lead to a deeper contentment.

Part Two

Discovering God

We have looked at the 5 habits.

They are the five things Adam started to do after God created him in his own image. We are like this because God is like this.

So if we do these five things we are being truly ourselves.

If you have been trying these habits out as you were reading through Part One, I hope you have been experiencing a new joy and a new contentment.

As a believer in Jesus, I am convinced that everyone is made in God's image, whether they believe in his existence or not. In other words, the habits work for everyone, whatever they believe or don't believe.

But people have said things like this to me: *I can see that these habits work; what I didn't realise is that there's stuff like this in the Bible.*

Maybe that's where *you* are. You can see that the habits work, and you want to find out if God's there or not.

Well, the best way to do that is to look at Jesus.

I want to make something clear. It's not that I believe in Jesus because I believe in God; it's the other way round. I believe in God because I am convinced by the historical evidence about Jesus.

And while the Bible says that every human being is made *in* God's image, it also says that Jesus is different: he *is* the image of God (Colossians 1:15; Hebrews 1:3).

So if we want to find out if God exists we need to look at Jesus.

The reason is simple.

The Christian claim is that Jesus is God revealing himself in human form. And that seems to me to be logical.

Imagine that there are 3 insects on my hand: they are discussing whether I exist.

Imagine that I love these insects; that I want to show myself to them so they can enjoy friendship with me; and that I can do anything I want.

What is the best way for me to show myself to them?

I could shout at them. Or I could squash them.

But there's a better way...

I could become an insect and live among them. They would notice that I'm different, and I could introduce myself to them.

The example of the insects doesn't *prove* anything.

But it shows that *if* God exists, *if* he made us to be his friends and *if* he wanted to show himself to us, it is logical that he should come into our world as a human being.

And that is what the Bible says he's done.

If we expect to see the 5 habits in Jesus' life, we're right.

He enjoyed beauty. He imagined the majestic robes of King Solomon; he talked about the beauty of flowers; he appreciated beautiful actions. (See Matthew 6:28-29; Mark 14:6)

He dug his garden. Jesus didn't stay at home: instead he travelled all over Israel with his message of forgiveness and of relationship with God. And he did all that on foot, which means he was looking after his body. (See Matthew 8:19-20; Matthew 15:21 and 29)

He practised self-control. When confronted with the confusion of his disciples or aware of the plotting of his enemies, Jesus didn't lash out: alongside his straight talking he continued to love friend and foe alike. (See Mark 8:14-21; Matthew 23:37-39)

He was creative. Jesus used stories, which is a very creative way of teaching. And many of his miracles involved him creating new things. (See Luke 15; Luke 7:36-50; Matthew 9:18-33)

He embraced others. If you watch how Jesus relates to people in the Gospel accounts you will see how he treated others with respect and compassion, especially those on the margins of society.
(See Mark 5:25-34; Mark 1:40-42)

But the Bible says that Jesus did not only come to show what God is like. He also came to bring us into a relationship with God so that we can know and experience him.

For anyone considering the claims of Christianity, here are 4 things about Jesus it is worth thinking about...

1. the life he lived
The Gospel records tell us that Jesus lived a life which made people think. As *the man for others*, he was constantly reaching out to others in love – and people noticed this. Despite his claim to be God in human form, he was humble and gentle.
(See John 10:30; 14:9; 11:36; 13:3-5; Luke 4:18-19)

2. the reason he died
Jesus told his disciples that he would suffer and die and that this *must* happen, because it was God's will.

But he also explained *why* he had to die: in dying on the cross he would pay the price to set sinners free.

The Christian claim is that we can be forgiven not because of what we do for God, but because of what God did for us, when Jesus died on the cross.

This is the reason Jesus died.
(See John 10:11; Mark 8:31; Mark 10:45)

3. the proof he succeeded
Jesus told his disciples that he would conquer death by rising to life three days after his crucifixion.

The New Testament says that in the resurrection God was declaring that the cross had worked: Jesus really had paid the price for our sins so that we could be forgiven.

So starting to follow Jesus is not a leap in the dark: by the resurrection God has told us what he thinks of what Jesus did on the cross.
(See Mark 14:28; Acts 10:39-43)

4. the gifts he offers

Because of his life, death and resurrection, Jesus is inviting us to put our trust in him, to decide to follow him.

And if we do, he will give us astonishing gifts. Let me just mention three.

First, he offers us forgiveness. Because Jesus took the punishment for my sins on the cross I can be forgiven.

Second, he offers us meaning. Because Jesus is God in human form I discover that the meaning of life is to live with him as the centre of everything I do.

Third, he offers us company. When someone turns from everything they know to be wrong to put their trust in Jesus, God the Holy Spirit comes to live in that person's life. That means they can begin to experience the presence of Jesus.
(See Luke 24:45-47; John 17:3; John 14:15-18)

This is not theory for me: this describes my life since I became a Christian.

It may be that you have reasons for not believing this stuff. But if Part Two has intrigued you and you want to take this further, please read Appendix 1.

I am convinced that the way to discover God is to get to know Jesus.

Part Three

Discovering the Missing Habit

God made us to be content.

In Part One we looked at how God made human beings in his own image. We saw that we are most contented when we live that out in practice.

From Genesis chapter 2 we saw what that means: Adam did 5 things because he was in God's image. And if these things become habits in *our* lives we will experience more contentment, because we will be *being truly ourselves*.

Here's a reminder of what the 5 habits are:

Enjoy beauty
Dig your garden
Practise self-control
Be creative
Embrace others

In Part Two we looked at Jesus, who *is* the image of God. And we saw that because he died on the cross we can be forgiven and come to discover God for ourselves.

A Christian is someone who has turned from their sin and opened their life up to Jesus.

And now, *in Part Three*, I want to introduce you to what I call the missing habit. There is another habit of Adam's which doesn't strike you at first; but once you see it it's obvious.

The missing habit is to *spend time with God*.

Read the Bible

Genesis chapter 2 is full of it.

God creates Adam (7) and puts him in a garden (8, 15). Then God talks to Adam (16) and brings the animals to him and talks to him again (19).

Do you see what's happening here?

God and Adam are *relating* to each other: there's a friendship here between the Creator and the human being he has made.

The Bible says that this contact has been broken through our sin: this rebellion against God began in Genesis chapter 3 but is something all of us are involved in. That's the reason I didn't include this habit in Part One.

But through Jesus the contact has been re-established: everyone who trusts in Jesus and his death on the cross is able to relate to God again, because the sin problem has been dealt with.

So if you are a believer in Jesus please do spend time with God.

Think it through

So as you practise the 5 habits of deeply contented people, *talk to God about them.*

Enjoy beauty. When you are enjoying the beauty of a favourite piece of music or of lakes and mountains, thank God for what you are experiencing. Share it with him!

Dig your garden. As you tidy your kitchen or go for a walk, talk to God about it: ask for his help and thank him for the joy you feel.

Practise self-control. When you are aware of something you need to say *No* to, ask God for help from the Holy Spirit; and thank him for the help you experience.

Be creative. If you are not sure of where your creative gifts lie, ask God to help you discover them. And thank God for the joy you experience as you exercise creativity.

Embrace others. Thank God for the people you know and ask him to help you show them that you love and respect them. Thank him for the pleasure of contact with others.

This is the missing habit: talking to and relating to the God we have come to know through Jesus.

Doubtless you noticed that gratitude to God is a big part of this. Someone once said that a problem atheists have is that they have no one to thank! Well, if we have discovered God by trusting in Jesus, that problem has been solved.

In one of his letters in the New Testament Paul tells his readers to *pray continually* (1 Thessalonians 5:17). That's great advice. Instead of talking to God *occasionally* we can talk to him *continually*.

Which means doing two things at once! I hope you will try it.

Try it out

Habit 6: Something to do

In what way are you *enjoying beauty*? Are you sharing your joy with God?

In what way are you *digging your garden*? Are you talking to God about this?

In what way are you *practising self-control*? Are you telling God about your areas of struggle and asking for his help? You might ask a friend to pray for you as you put this habit into practice.

Are you *being creative*? Are you asking God to help you and sharing your joy with him?

And are you *embracing others*? Are you thanking God for the people in your life?

And will you relate to God by trying to *pray continually*?

This habit of relating to God is missing from the lives of some people who have been Christians for many years. I know this because sometimes it has been missing from my life, too.

It was a massive step forward for me when I realised that this habit is not just a matter of reading the Bible once a day and spending a few minutes praying in the morning or the evening.

We saw it in Part Two: when we discover God when we decide to trust and follow Jesus, the Holy Spirit comes in and lives in our personality. We may feel this at once, or the feelings may come later.

But he is there.

This means that I can talk to God at any time, whatever I am doing. I am praying for you as I write this paragraph, that if you are a Christian you will find yourself talking to God again and again through the day.

This is wonderfully possible for two reasons: first, because Jesus has taken away the barrier between us and God by dying on the cross for our sins. And, second, because the Holy Spirit is now living inside us.

Developing the missing habit / Habit 6: Something to do

If you are a Christian, please try to make a time every day to read the Bible and to talk to God about the world, your friends and your life.

But please try, too, to develop the habit of talking to God *while you are doing other things*. So you could be praying while walking to the bus stop or talking to a friend.

This needs practice, but the Holy Spirit wants to help you to do this.

As we discover and develop the missing habit of relating to God we will experience a deeper contentment.

Conclusion

The Experience of Contentment

So all of us are looking for contentment.

And of course there will be lots of different ways we look for it: some will get us somewhere and others will be dead ends.

Because we are all different there will be some things which work for you but which don't work for me.

But if the Bible is telling us the truth (and I am convinced that it is), then the habits we have found in Genesis chapter 2 will increase the contentment of anyone who puts them to the test.

This is because we will be actively living out what it means to be human beings made in God's image.

I am not claiming that this will abolish all our struggles! We all have different starting points. Some of us will need help from a counsellor or a doctor.

But all of us will benefit from trying to incorporate the habits into our own lives.

And if Jesus really *is* the image of God – God in human form – (and I'm convinced that he is), then his decision to go to the cross to put us right with God is astonishing love.

And our decision to put him at the centre of our lives is one of the sanest we will ever make. The Bible is right.

> *Godliness with contentment is great gain.*
>
> 1 Timothy 6:6

The God who made us wants us to experience this. A deeper level of contentment is within our grasp.

Appendix 1

Discovering God: what now?

If you have read *Part Two: Discovering God*, it's possible that you want to take this further.

If that's where you are, Appendix 1 is for you.

1. If you have objections or questions

You will find it helpful to go to a *Christianity Explored* course (christianity explored.org) or an *Alpha* course (alpha.org). There is plenty of opportunity for discussion and questions.

Ask around and someone will point you in the right direction.

2. If you believe the message of Jesus

Maybe the 4 things about Jesus make sense to you:

the life he lived
Do you believe Jesus lived an amazing life which showed that he was God in human form?

the reason he died
Do you believe that he died on the cross in order to pay the price for our sins?

the proof he succeeded
Do you believe that the proof he paid for our sins is that he rose from the dead?

the gifts he offers
Do you believe that he is offering you gifts of forgiveness, meaning and company?

If the answer to all these questions is *Yes,* you are ready to become a Christian, which means turning from sin and trusting in Jesus.

When I took this step myself I prayed a prayer similar to the one below. Millions of people have responded to the good news about Jesus by praying something like this. Read it through first; then, if you know you are ready, pray it slowly and thoughtfully, adding other words if they occur to you.

Jesus, who is the image of God, is listening.

A prayer for anyone who has discovered God in Jesus

the life he lived
Lord Jesus, I believe that you are the eternal Son of God. Thank you for coming into this world and showing us what God is like. Thank you for your love for everyone you met.

the reason he died
I know that I don't live with you at the centre of everything. Here are some of the sins in my life I'm aware of...

Lord Jesus, thank you for going to the cross. Thank you that when you died you were in my place, taking the punishment for my sin, so that I could be forgiven.

the proof he succeeded
Thank you that I know you paid the price for my sins because you rose from the dead. Thank you that you're alive and you are hearing what I say to you now...

the gifts he offers
Thank you for your invitation to receive you and your gifts. Lord Jesus, I now turn from everything I know to be wrong.

Please come into my life by your Holy Spirit and give me the forgiveness you earned for me on the cross; please come into my life and let me experience meaning as I know you; and please come into my life and let me experience your company.

Lord Jesus, thank you that you have come in and are now living in me. Here are some things I want to thank you for...

Amen.

If you have prayed this prayer and meant it, a miracle has happened!

You have become a Christian: you are a son or a daughter of God, you are forgiven completely because Jesus died for you on the cross, God's Holy Spirit is living inside you and after this life is over you will be with him for ever.

You have always been in God's image; but now, because you are trusting Jesus, you are in his family, too.

I hope you will keep using the habits, and include Habit 6 (see Part Three).

And there are some other things you can do, too.

Please *read the Bible*. Most people aren't used to this. But the Bible is the main way in which God speaks to us. Why not read half a chapter of Mark's Gospel every day?

Please *tell a friend*. This is not about preaching at people! But it *is* about being willing to tell people who mean something to us about what God has done in our lives.

And please *find a church*. Find one where people love Jesus and are excited about the fact that he died on the cross for sinners. You will see this in the songs they sing, in the lives they lead, and in the way they expect God to speak to them through the Bible.

If you would like to write to me, I would love to hear from you:
andrew@themarkdrama.com.

Appendix 2

The 6 Habits in a Small Group

The following series of studies lasts 7 weeks and is designed for group use. That might be a church house-group, or two friends meeting up to talk through the habits together. It would help if everyone had a copy of *The 5 Habits of Deeply Contented People* and a Bible.

Two hints for group leaders

a)   It may be good if you say a short prayer at the beginning of your time together. And perhaps the group will want to pray together at the end.

b)   Try to take a little time between sessions to pray for each member of the group.

Week One
Habit 1: Enjoy beauty

1.   Turn to Genesis chapter 2. Does anyone remember which bits of the chapter show that Eden was beautiful and that Adam enjoyed it?

2.   What is there in Genesis to make us think that God, too, was enjoying the beauty of what he had created?

3.   What are some of the ways that we have been *enjoying beauty* before we ever read this book? How did you first discover that you enjoyed this kind of beauty? What effect does it have on you? How does it make you feel?

4.   Have any of us discovered any new ways of *enjoying beauty* since we read about this first habit? If we are glad that we have tried this out, why is that?

5.   How often are we managing to *enjoy beauty*?

Week Two
Habit 2: Dig your garden

1. Where does the writer of Genesis tell us that God gave this task to Adam? How do we think Adam felt about this?

2. Is there any indication that God had *worked* to make everything?

3. Would anyone like to tell us in what way they *dig their garden* at home? Does it make you feel good when you do it? Would you recommend this to the rest of us?

4. Imagine that a friend doesn't think this would work at all. If we wanted to convince them, how might we do it?

5. Can we think of any other ways of *digging our garden* which are not mentioned in the book?

Week Three
Habit 3: Practise self-control

1. Where in Genesis chapter 2 does God put Adam in a situation where he wants him to be self-controlled? Would we describe God here in a positive or in a negative way? Do we think that *God* is self-controlled?

2. Share with one another some areas of life in which you find it easy to be self-controlled. How does it make you feel when you are?

3. Try to think of examples from the news which show that someone has had zero self-control. How do you feel about that person?

4. Does anyone want to share with the rest of us an area where we find it hard to be self-controlled? How can we support you as a group?

5. Can we think of things that will help us to see this third habit as a *positive* thing?

Week Four
Habit 4: Be creative

1. Why do we think God decided to ask Adam what he wanted to call the animals in verse 19 of Genesis chapter 2?

2. Do we agree that lots of people think they're *not* creative? Are they right or wrong?

3. Would any of us like to share in what ways they think they're creative? How did you discover this? What kind of creativity do we see in one another?

4. Can any of us think of new areas in which we'd like to find out if we're creative or not?

5. How does being creative make us *feel*?

Week Five
Habit 5: Embrace others

1. How do we think the Bible shows us that God wants relationship?

2. In Genesis chapter 2 this habit applies to marriage. Do we think that broadening it out to other people is pushing it a bit?

3. Can we think of examples of how we can *embrace others* if they are work colleagues or strangers?

4. Would any of us like to share ways in which we have *embraced others* in a new way since reading the book? What was the effect on the other person? And how did It make *you* feel?

5. How would you help someone struggling with loneliness to give this habit a try?

Week Six
Habit 6: Relate to God

1. Turn to Genesis chapter 2. Where do we see here that God and Adam are relating to each other? How do we think this felt for Adam? And for God?

2.   What is it that prevents many people enjoying a relationship with God? In what way does the cross make a difference?

3.   Can we give some examples of when we have found ourselves thanking God when using one of the 5 habits?

4.   How do we get on with doing two things at once (ie talking to God while we are doing something else)? Or have we given up trying?!?

5.   When we do manage to talk to God many times during the day, what difference does that make to us?

Week Seven
Living the 6 habits

1.   Which of the 6 habits do we find the hardest to put into practice? Why?

2.   Which of the habits are we enjoying most? Why?

3.   Does the idea of living like people made in God's image excite us or not? Why?/Why not?

4.   How much do we think we were using these habits before we started reading this book? Has it been a help to use them more deliberately?

5.   As you have been thinking about the habits of deeply contented people, what's the most important discovery you have made?

How to Teach the Bible so that People Meet God

Andrew Page

Andrew Page believes that Bible teaching can be a supernatural event. A graduate of London School of Theology, Andrew was a missionary in Austria for 20 years, working with the Austrian Christian student movement (IFES) and later pastoring a church in Innsbruck.

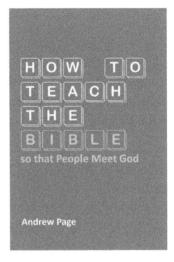

He says "Two enemies of Christian churches are Bible teaching with little biblical content and Bible teaching which is more a lecture than an event." If you agree with this, *How to Teach the Bible so that People Meet God* is the book for you.

This is unashamedly a how-to book. Andrew has trained others in this method of teaching a Bible passage in a number of countries around Europe, and now for the first time the method is available as a book.

So, 3 questions before you buy this book:
- Do you want to find out if God has given you the gift of teaching?
- Do you want to grow in the gift you believe you have?
- Do you want to help a friend to develop as a Bible teacher?

If you have said *Yes* to any of these questions, *How to Teach the Bible so that People Meet God* is a great place to start.

ISBN 978-3-95776-035-7
Pb. • 90 pp. • £ 7.50

VTR Publications
info@vtr-online.com
http://www.vtr-online.com

The Mark Experiment

How Mark's Gospel can help you know Jesus better

Andrew Page

If you are looking for a new way into Mark's Gospel and you long to allow the Gospel to help you worship and experience Jesus, *The Mark Experiment* is the book for you.

In *The Mark Experiment* Andrew Page shows you how to commit the Gospel to memory and explains how learning to meditate on the Gospel events has transformed his relationship with Jesus. Think what this might mean for your understanding of the life and ministry of Jesus.

One exciting result of this book has been the development of an innovative drama in which a team of 15 Christians from a church or student group acts out every incident in the Gospel of Mark as theatre-in-the-round. The Mark Drama is now being performed in many countries around the world.

www.themarkdrama.com

ISBN 978-3-937965-21-5
Pb. • 106 pp. • £ 8.00

VTR Publications
info@vtr-online.com
http://www.vtr-online.com

Lightning Source UK Ltd.
Milton Keynes UK
UKHW020633260920
370569UK00006B/172

9 783957 760098